"What I like most about your book are the love letters from God. It's almost like He's right there in my room talking to me, like He knows me so well. I like the part about being a blessing, and that I am a beautiful creation to Him. I really like the book and I would like one of the first copies when it comes out!"

—OLIVIA, AGE 9

"Thanks, Sheri Rose. I can't tell you how much of an impact your book had on Olivia. She read a little bit each night before bed and had a hard time putting it down! Isabella, who's seven and a half, liked it very much as well—her smile each night spoke a thousand words. The book is so positive and affirming. It accurately communicates the true character of our loving God."

—ROBIN

"*His Little Princess* teaches me that I am not a pretend princess, but a real one! And it teaches me that to God I am beautiful, no matter what! This book has helped me a lot. Even though I sometimes make bad choices, I know that God still loves me. And I'm not afraid at night anymore. Thank you for writing this book. It has been a big step in my life!"

—ELIZABETH, AGE 8

"These love letters are great, and I want them for my granddaughters. What a captivating, wonderful book! We are created to bring beauty. You have so captured this in *His Little Princess*."

—LEE ANNE

His Little Princess

This book is presented to:

Juliette, Amari, Jenavieve
a. Sahfia

Love,
mommy

Dedicated to my gift from God—
my daughter,
Emilee Joy Shepherd

His Little Princess

Treasured Letters from Your King

Sheri Rose SHEPHERD

Illustrations by Lisa Marie Browning

Multnomah Books

HIS LITTLE PRINCESS
published by Multnomah Books
A division of Random House, Inc.
© 2006 by Sheri Rose Shepherd
International Standard Book Number: 1-59052-601-5

Illustrations by Lisa Marie Browning
Cover and interior design by Katherine Lloyd, The DESK

Multnomah is a trademark of Multnomah Publishers
and is registered in the U.S. Patent and Trademark Office.
The colophon is a trademark of Multnomah Publishers.
Printed in China

For information:
MULTNOMAH BOOKS
12265 ORACLE BOULEVARD, SUITE 200
COLORADO SPRINGS, CO 80921

07 08 09 10 11—10 9 8 7 6 5 4 3

Letters from the King

Do Not Give Up
Do Not Tease
In Times of Sickness
Angels Watching Over You
Honor the Elderly
Dress like Royalty
Friends Are a Gift
Sweet Dreams, My Love
Christmas Day
My Word Is True
Try, Try Again
Always Do Your Best
A Princess Does Not Brag
Love People the Way I Do
Meet Me at Church
Have Faith, My Child
Do Not Be Jealous
My Patient Princess
Telling the Truth
Jesus Died for You
Telling People About Jesus
Open Your Gift
Presents in Heaven
Death Is Not the End
A Home in Heaven

Prayers from the Princess

Thank You for Choosing Me
I Love You Too, Lord
Thank You for Making Me
Help Me to Have a Good Attitude
I Want an Unselfish Heart
Teach Me How to Show Respect
I Want to Make Good Choices
Forgive Me, Lord
Help Me to Trust in You
Give Me Beautiful Lips
Help Me Not to Be Afraid
Heal My Heart
I Love Your World
Teach Me to Bless Others
Help Me to Be Strong
I Will Praise You, Lord
Teach Me to Be Like You
Help Me to Love My Family
Help Me When I'm Angry
I Am Sorry, Lord
A Prayer for My Parents
Keep Me from Evil
When I Am Hurting
Teach Me to Speak Kindly
Put a Song in My Heart

I Want to Always Be Your Girl
Lord, Change My Heart
You Are My Healer
Send Your Angels to Protect Me
Help Me to Honor My Grandparents
Dress Me like a Princess
I Want to Be a Good Friend
You Are My Light in the Night
Merry Christmas, Father!
I Love to Read the Bible
I Will Trust in You
Help Me to Do My Best
I Will Not Boast or Brag
You Made Us All
I Love Your Church
Strengthen My Faith
Forgive Me for Being Jealous
Give Me Patience, Father
I Will Not Tell a Lie
Come into My Heart, Jesus
I Want to Spread the Good News
Thank You for My Gift
You See Everything I Do
Comfort Me, Lord
Happily Ever After

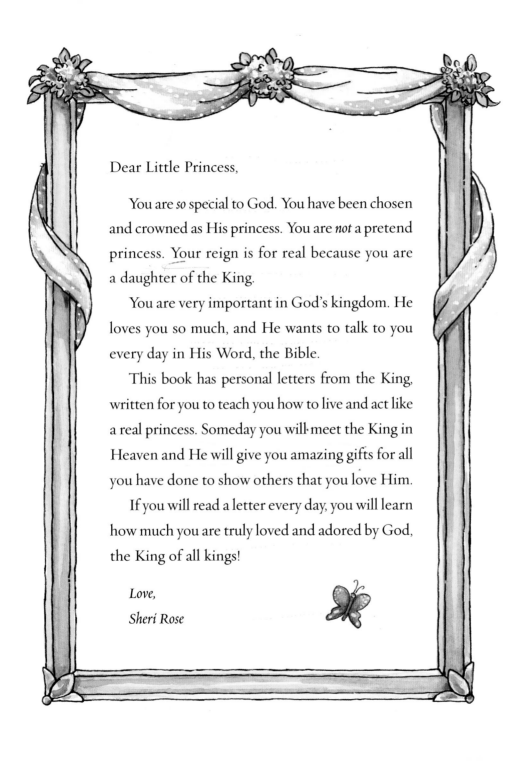

Dear Little Princess,

You are *so* special to God. You have been chosen and crowned as His princess. You are *not* a pretend princess. Your reign is for real because you are a daughter of the King.

You are very important in God's kingdom. He loves you so much, and He wants to talk to you every day in His Word, the Bible.

This book has personal letters from the King, written for you to teach you how to live and act like a real princess. Someday you will meet the King in Heaven and He will give you amazing gifts for all you have done to show others that you love Him.

If you will read a letter every day, you will learn how much you are truly loved and adored by God, the King of all kings!

Love,
Sheri Rose

I Chose You, My Princess

My Chosen Daughter,

You are not a pretend princess, my child. You are a real princess, and I am your God, the King of all kings. I chose you before you were even born to be my princess. You are very important in my kingdom. I have chosen you to do something special that only you can do. I have amazing plans for you, both now and for when you grow up. Remember, a crown and a palace do not make you a true princess—it is your love for me and for others that will make you special. If you read my words every day in the Bible, I will teach you all you need to know about living like a daughter of the King.

Love,
Your King and Father in Heaven

"You didn't choose me. I chose you."

JOHN 15:16

Thank You for Choosing Me

Dear God, thank you for choosing me to be your princess. I feel so special knowing I belong to you. Help me to remember to act like I am yours, because I need help. I'm glad you are my King who can make me shine for you! I pray in Jesus' name, amen.

My Amazing Love for You

Dear Precious Daughter,

I am your Daddy in Heaven, and I love you so much! I know you have a daddy on earth too—I created him, just as I created you. But I am the God of all Heaven and earth, and I am your King and you are my daughter. You are precious to me in every way. I think about you all the time. Nothing is more important to me than you. I want you to tuck this truth in your heart: No matter how big you grow or where you go, you'll always be my girl and I will always be your God. I will always love you, no matter what you do, and I will never leave you!

Love,
Your King who will never stop loving you

....

"I have loved you with a love that lasts forever."

JEREMIAH 31:3, NIRV

I Love You Too, Lord

Dear God, I'm so happy that you love me. Thank you for all you've done for me. Thank you that I get to be with you always. Thank you for your promise that you will never leave me. In Jesus' name I pray, amen.

I Made You Beautiful

My Pretty Little Princess,

I want you to know how very beautiful you are to me. I adore you, my daughter! I love the way I created you. When you look into the mirror, remember that I carefully chose the color of your eyes and the highlights in your hair. I love you so much that I know exactly how many hairs are on your pretty little head! I designed the shape of your nose and your happy smile. I made every part of your precious body. Don't ever try to look like anyone else but you. I think you're perfect just the way you are. I love every little thing about you, my princess. There is no one in the world like you.

Love,
Your King who created a perfect you

....

You are the one who put me together inside my mother's body, and I praise you because of the wonderful way you created me. Everything you do is marvelous! Of this I have no doubt.

PSALM 139:13–14, CEV

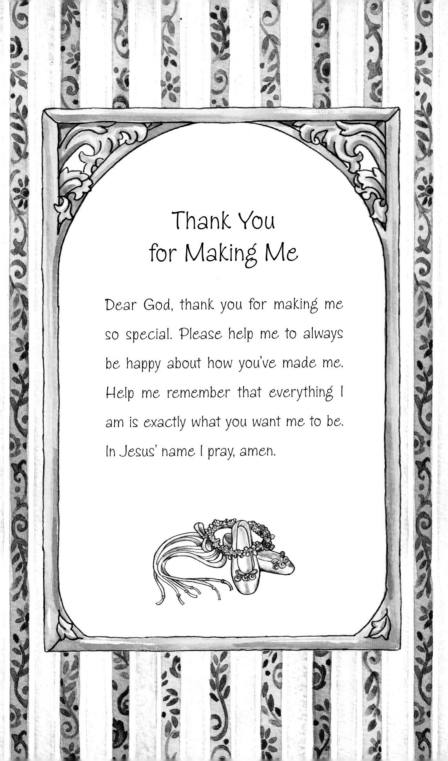

Thank You for Making Me

Dear God, thank you for making me so special. Please help me to always be happy about how you've made me. Help me remember that everything I am is exactly what you want me to be. In Jesus' name I pray, amen.

The Attitude of a Princess

Dearest Child,

A princess of mine needs to keep a good attitude and a tender heart. My love, it is easy to have a good attitude when you get what you want or when you're having a good day. It gets hard when bad days happen or when you cannot have something you really want. Remember, it is impossible for you to act like my daughter without my help. Just like you, every girl in the Bible who did great things for my kingdom needed my help. So when you feel mad or hurt or disappointed, come to me and ask me to give you a heart that will show everyone you are mine. And I will help you keep a good attitude.

Love,
Your King and your helper

Above all else, guard your heart,
for it affects everything you do.

PROVERBS 4:23

Help Me to Have
a Good Attitude

Dear God, sometimes I have a bad attitude and I don't act like your princess. Please forgive me. I need you to help me act like the princess you have chosen me to be. Help me remember that my Daddy is the King of all kings. In Jesus' name I pray, amen.

My Unselfish Princess

My Dear Daughter,

Today I will teach you how to become truly beautiful. As you learn how to act like my princess, you'll discover that giving and sharing feels so much better than taking from others and demanding that you get your own way. Remember, my love, it is easy to think only about what *you* want; but if you want everyone to know that you are my princess, then you will need the unselfish heart of a princess. You will need to do the things I ask you to do, even if it means not getting just what you want at the moment. Every time you choose to be unselfish, you make my heart happy.

Love,
Your King who teaches you to give

Whatever you eat or drink or whatever you do,
you must do all for the glory of God.

1 Corinthians 10:31

I Want an Unselfish Heart

Dear God, it's really hard for me to share my things and to think about others before I think about myself. I need you to change my heart. Help me remember that I am showing others your love by thinking of them first. In Jesus' name I pray, amen.

Showing Respect

Dearest Princess of Mine,

This is an important lesson, my daughter, so pay close attention to my words. Respect is a very important part of being my princess. You can show respect in many different ways. When you follow the rules at school, you are showing respect to your teachers. When you quietly listen as others are speaking, you are showing them respect too. When you obey your parents, you are showing that you love and respect them. Every time you show respect to others, I'm so proud because you are acting like my girl. I will love you no matter how you act, but I created you to treat others with respect—just as I want others to honor and respect you.

Love,
Your King whom you love and obey

....

Show respect for everyone. Love your Christian brothers and sisters. Fear God. Show respect for the king.

1 PETER 2:17

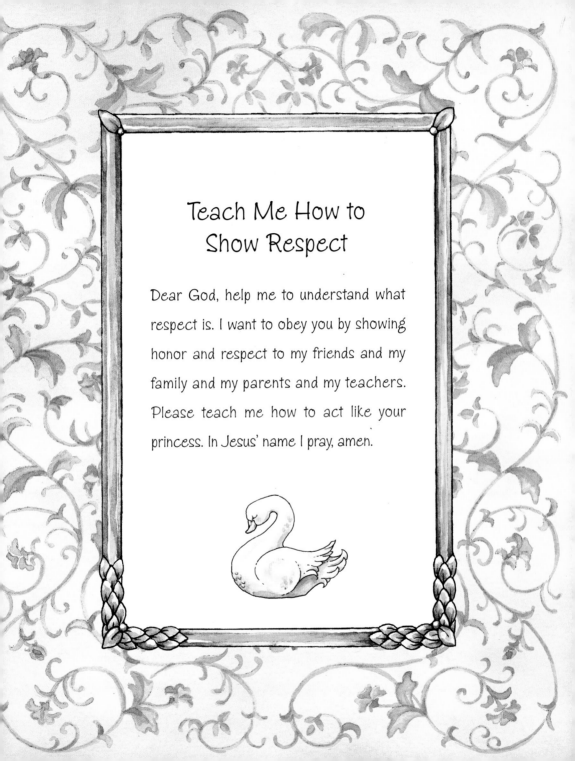

Teach Me How to Show Respect

Dear God, help me to understand what respect is. I want to obey you by showing honor and respect to my friends and my family and my parents and my teachers. Please teach me how to act like your princess. In Jesus' name I pray, amen.

Making Good Choices

My Precious Princess,

When you make good choices, you show others that you love me. I love you no matter what you do or how you behave, but when you choose to disobey me, you can hurt yourself and others. And I don't want you to get hurt. I did not give you a list of rules to stop you from having fun or to make your life hard. I wrote to you in my Bible the secret to having joy in your heart. If you will choose to hear and obey my words, I will do things for you that are bigger than you could ever imagine! Remember, I will always be here to help you make the right choices.

Love,
Your King who chose you

....

"If they listen and obey God, then they will be blessed with prosperity throughout their lives. All their years will be pleasant."

JOB 36:11

I Want to Make Good Choices

Dear God, I want to make you proud of me. I want to make good choices and act in a way that shows others I am a daughter of the King. Please help me hear you and obey. I love you. In Jesus' name I pray, amen.

I Will Always Forgive You

Dear Princess,

You can talk to me about anything—even the things in your heart that are not pretty. I want you to tell me when you make a bad choice or hurt someone's feelings. I will always forgive you, and I will never stop loving you. No one is perfect, not even grown-ups who love me. That is why I sent my only Son, Jesus, to die on the cross, so you would not have to be perfect to get to Heaven someday. Now take a moment and think about your day. Is there anything you need to confess or tell me? Anything you have done wrong, I will make right in Heaven because I love you so much.

Love,
Your King who loves to talk with you

....

But if we confess our sins to God, he can
always be trusted to forgive us and take our sins away.

1 JOHN 1:9, CEV

Forgive Me, Lord

Dear God, help me remember the things I've done and said that I need to be forgiven for. Thank you that I can tell you anything that is in my heart, no matter how bad it seems. Thank you that you always forgive me when I ask. In Jesus' name I pray, amen.

Talk with Me, My Princess

My Chosen Child,

I want you to know you can talk to me anytime about anything. Tell your Daddy in Heaven when you are sad or glad or need my help. Nothing is too big or too small for your God. I love to hear your prayers and I am waiting to answer them, my love. Many times I will give you exactly what you ask for, and sometimes I won't do things your way because I know what is best for my girl. But you can always trust me to take care of your needs. Your little prayers are big in Heaven, and I hear every one of them. I am always here for you, my princess.

Love,
Your King who hears your prayers

Yes, ask anything in my name,
and I will do it!

JOHN 14:14

Help Me to Trust in You

Dear God, help me to believe that you hear me when I pray. Please help me to trust you when I don't see you answer my prayers right away or in just the way I want you to. You know what's best for me. In Jesus' name I pray, amen.

A Princess's Words

Dear Princess,

Be careful what you say. I want your words to be a gift to anyone who talks with you. I have given you beautiful lips to talk like a princess. The things you say should help people feel happy in their heart. When you talk, speak sweetly and kindly. If someone is sad, you can help them feel better by praying for them or just by saying something kind. If someone does not feel loved, you can tell them I love them. Remember, my love, you may be the only person to tell that person about me. Remember that you are my princess and use your words to make your friends and family feel special.

Love,
Your King who loves your words

....

Watch the way you talk. Let nothing foul or dirty come out of your mouth. Say only what helps, each word a gift.

EPHESIANS 4:29, THE MESSAGE

Give Me Beautiful Lips

Dear God, please make my lips pretty by helping me to speak words that are kind and sweet. I am sorry for the times I have not talked like your daughter. Please forgive me and give me words that will tell others I am yours. In Jesus' name I pray, amen.

Fear Not, My Child

My Daughter,

I know that sometimes you feel afraid. Even grown-ups feel afraid sometimes. When you are scared or afraid, tell me and I will help you feel safe. I am with you all the time, and I will never leave you alone, my love. Just as I protected my child Daniel in the lions' den, I will keep you safe, my princess, no matter where you are. I will send my angels to protect you because I am your God. I care about every little thing that frightens you, so talk to me when you are scared. I will always be here for you, little one. Do not let your heart be afraid of anything!

Love,
Your King who always protects you

....

"My God sent his angel to shut the lions' mouths
so that they would not hurt me."

Daniel 6:22

Help Me Not to Be Afraid

Dear God, sometimes I feel so afraid and it's hard for me to believe you are with me when I cannot see you. Please help me like you helped Daniel when he was afraid of the lions. Help me to feel you near me when I am afraid. In Jesus' name I pray, amen.

When You Are Disappointed

Dear Princess,

Sometimes sad things happen. Life will not always go the way you want it to. Sometimes people will do or say things that hurt your feelings. When this happens, it's okay to feel sad and disappointed. Even I have felt disappointment, my love. I know how hard it is to act like my princess when your heart is hurting. It's okay to cry. Just know that I am here for you when you are hurting and I can make your heart happy again. But it may take some time before you feel better, so stay close to me when you're sad or disappointed. I will help you keep a princess heart, and I will give you joy while you're healing.

Love,
Your King and your joy

....

Those who plant in tears will harvest with shouts of joy.

PSALM 126:5

Heal My Heart

Dear God, some days a lot of things hurt my feelings—it's hard to act like your princess when I am sad. Please heal my heart and make me happy inside again. Help me remember that you will never leave me and that you'll always love me. In Jesus' name I pray, amen.

My Beautiful Creation

Dear Priceless Daughter,

When you see a beautiful flower, or feel a cool summer breeze on your sweet little face, I am showing you how much I love you. I created all this beauty for you to enjoy! I send rain to make the flowers grow. I give you sunshine to warm your toes on a summer's day. I send birds to sing to you and animals for you to love and care for. I make the stars sparkle like diamonds just for you. Did you know that *you* are my *favorite* creation? You are my little girl and I made all these very special things to make you happy. Look around and see the way I colored the world just for you!

Love,
Your King who is the Creator of everything

....

You alone are the LORD, Creator of the heavens and all the stars, Creator of the earth and those who live on it, Creator of the ocean and all its creatures. You are the source of life, praised by the stars that fill the heavens.

NEHEMIAH 9:6, CEV

I Love Your World

Dear God, thank you for all the beautiful things you've made. Thank you for the breeze that cools my face and whispers that you love me. Thank you for all the wonderful stars in the sky. Thank you for making me to be me! In Jesus' name I pray, amen.

You Are a Blessing

Dear Princess,

A blessing is something you do or say that makes others feel loved. I want you to bless people whenever you can. When you see your mom working hard to clean the house, ask her what you can do to help. When you see your brother or sister trying to do something that is too hard for them, offer to help or even do it for them. Remember, my love, a true princess—my princess—thinks about others first. Look for ways every day to make someone feel loved. I have blessed you, my princess, so that you may bless others.

Love,
Your King who loves to bless you

She must also be well-known for doing all sorts of good things, such as raising children, giving food to strangers, welcoming God's people into her home, helping people in need, and always making herself useful.

1 TIMOTHY 5:10, CEV

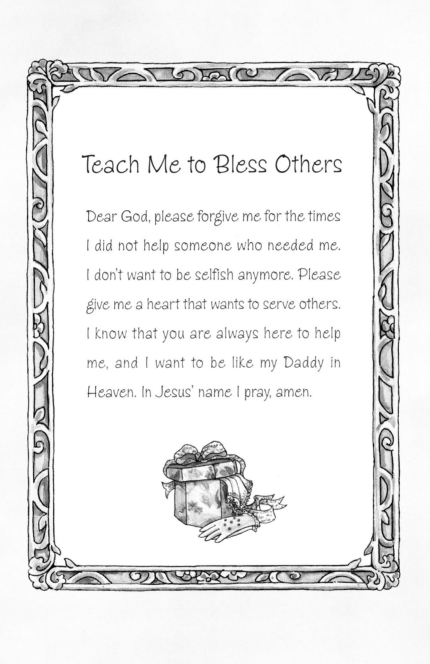

Teach Me to Bless Others

Dear God, please forgive me for the times I did not help someone who needed me. I don't want to be selfish anymore. Please give me a heart that wants to serve others. I know that you are always here to help me, and I want to be like my Daddy in Heaven. In Jesus' name I pray, amen.

Take Courage, My Princess

Dear Princess,

I will help you to have courage, my child, just as I helped Queen Esther. She didn't have a mommy or daddy to teach her how to be strong and courageous. But I was her Daddy in Heaven and she loved me very much, and she knew I would never leave her. I asked her to tell the king of the land not to hurt my people. Esther was scared, but she trusted me to give her the words to say when she stood before the king. Esther obeyed and she rescued my people. Today she is remembered for her great courage. Pray for courage and I will gladly give it to you when you need it.

Love,
Your King who is your strength

....

Esther answered, "Your Majesty, if you really care for me and are willing to help, you can save me and my people. That's what I really want."

ESTHER 7:3, CEV

Help Me to Be Strong

Dear God, I want to have the courage to say and do the right things, even when it's hard or I'm afraid. Please help me not be afraid to do whatever you ask me to. Thank you that you are always here to help me. I love you so much. In Jesus' name I pray, amen.

Worship Your King

Dear Precious Child,

Your voice fills my heart with joy! Did you know that when you sing of your love for me, all of Heaven is listening? You can praise me in the morning and in the nighttime before you go to bed. You can raise your beautiful voice to me anytime. Did you know that David, who killed the giant Goliath in battle, praised me all the time? I helped David do lots of special things for my kingdom because he loved me and he wrote many songs of praise to me. Princess, I chose you, just as I chose David. So sing your heart out, my love. I hear every word that comes from my daughter's mouth.

Love,
Your King who loves to hear you sing

I will praise you, Lord, with all my heart
and tell about the wonders you have worked.

PSALM 9:1, CEV

I Will Praise You, Lord

Dear God, I love to sing to you. It makes my heart happy when I sing songs about how much I love you and how much you love me. I will sing to you even when I grow up because I know you hear every word I sing from my heart. In Jesus' name I pray, amen.

The Character of a Princess

Dear Princess,

Today I want to teach you about the character of a true princess. Having character means doing the right thing when no one is looking. It means making a good choice when you do not want to. Character is like a very special treasure—it is a rare jewel that is very hard to find in some people. But you are my daughter and it is your character that will make you shine for me. If you ask, I will always help you do what is right in my sight. Remember, it is very hard to do anything without me. So ask me to give you the beauty of character and I will, my love.

Love,
Your King who makes you shine

....

"And now, my daughter, don't be afraid.
I will do for you all you ask. All my fellow townsmen know
that you are a woman of noble character."

RUTH 3:11, NIV

Teach Me to Be Like You

Dear God, I want to shine as your chosen princess. Please help me make good choices, even when I don't want to. Help me do the right thing, even when no one is watching. Help me become more and more like you. In Jesus' name I pray, amen.

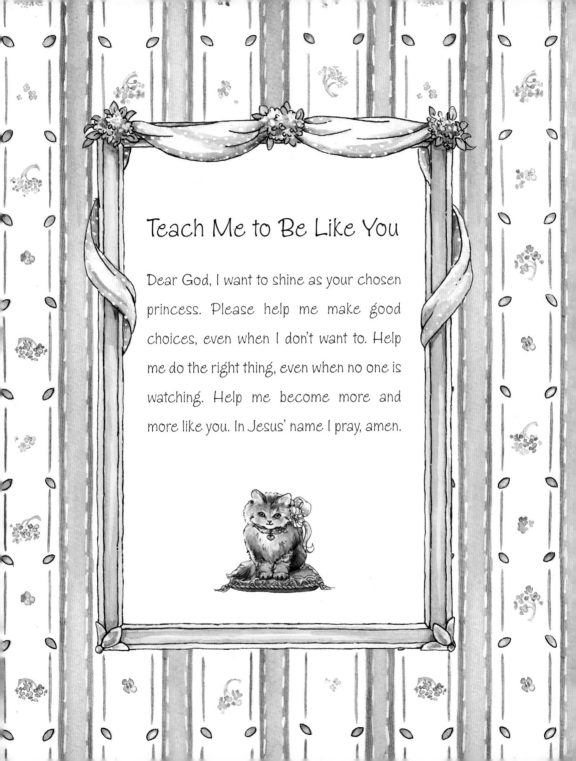

Love Your Family

Dear Beloved Daughter,

Show your family that you love them. I know this is sometimes hard to do. It takes a real princess heart (and a prayer) to love your family when a brother or sister hurts you or makes you mad. I know how it feels when people you love do things that break your heart. When I sent Jesus to love the people I created, many of them treated my Son cruelly. But I still loved them. Please know in your heart that I love you no matter how you act—and I am asking you to do the same for your family. Remember, no one will ever love you the way I do, because I am God and your King.

Love,
Your King who gave you a family to love

And here is how to measure it—the greatest love is shown
when people lay down their lives for their friends.

JOHN 15:13

Help Me to Love My Family

Dear God, help me to love my family.
Thank you that I'm in your family. Thank
you that you love me no matter what I do
or how I act. I love you, Lord, and I want to
learn to love others the way you love me.
In Jesus' name I pray, amen.

When You're Angry

Dearest Daughter,

Everybody gets angry sometimes. I have felt this way many times. But I will never get mad at you for feeling angry, my child. It is not a sin to become angry, but it is wrong for you to lash out in anger and hurt other people or yourself. When you feel mad or angry, tell me about it. You can even cry out to me as David did. I will always hear you. I love you and I care about everything that bothers you, my daughter. So come to your Daddy in Heaven with your troubles. I will heal your heart from anger and give you back a calm and happy heart full of love.

Love,

Your King who is always here for you

Don't get so angry that you sin. Don't go to bed angry.

EPHESIANS 4:26, CEV

Help Me When I'm Angry

Dear God, help me when I feel angry inside. Sometimes my friends or family make me really mad. I'm sorry for those times when I don't act like your daughter. Thank you for loving me anyway. In Jesus' name I pray, amen.

Saying You're Sorry

Dear Princess,

The words "I'm sorry" are like a treasure of love you can give to someone you have hurt. I know it can be hard to say you're sorry, especially when you did not mean to hurt someone. But I want you to help those you have hurt by telling them you're sorry. Remember this, my love: I will always forgive you right away. But sometimes the people you have hurt will take a long time to forgive you. When this happens I want you to pray for them, and in time I will help them forgive you. And I will bless you with a princess heart that finds joy in doing what is right.

Love,
Your King who always forgives you

....

But I confess my sins;
I am deeply sorry for what I have done.

PSALM 38:18

I Am Sorry, Lord

Dear God, sometimes I don't feel like saying I'm sorry, so I need you to help me do the right thing. Please help me say I'm sorry when I've hurt someone, and help them to forgive me. In Jesus' name I pray, amen.

A Parent's Protection

Dear Princess of Mine,

I gave you a mom and dad for your protection. They are like an umbrella on a stormy day in the rain—just as the umbrella keeps you from getting wet, your parents protect you from harm by setting rules for you to obey. Sometimes it's hard to be a parent. Raising a child is a very big responsibility. So I want you to honor your parents by being kind and obedient. It is the right thing to do, my daughter. You will make your King happy by treating your mom and dad with love and respect. Remember this, my princess: If you honor and obey your parents, I will bless you in a very special way as you grow.

Love,
Your King and Daddy in Heaven

....

Children, obey your parents because you belong to the Lord,
for this is the right thing to do.

Ephesians 6:1

A Prayer for My Parents

Dear God, thank you for my parents. Please help me to obey them, even when I want to do things my own way. Help my parents to take care of me and to teach me all about you. I'm glad that you are always there to help them. In Jesus' name I pray, amen.

Resist Temptation

Dear Daughter,

Beware! Because you are my chosen child, you have an enemy. He is the devil and he'll try to trick you into making bad choices. He will whisper to you things like "Do whatever *feels* right" and "You have every right to be angry." The devil tricked my first daughter, Eve, into disobeying me. She believed his lies and she sinned. I want you to come to me first when you're thinking about disobeying or doing something that you know in your heart is wrong. I will help you to be strong and do the right thing. But if you do fall down by making a bad choice, come to me and I will help you get back up again.

Love,
Your King who makes you strong

....

Keep alert and pray.
Otherwise temptation will overpower you.

MARK 14:38

Keep Me from Evil

Dear God, lots of times it's hard for me to do or say the right thing. Please help me to see when the devil is trying to trick me into disobeying. Protect me from evil and help me remember to pray when I'm being tempted. Help me to hear your voice in my heart. In Jesus' name I pray, amen.

I Was Also Rejected

Dear Daughter,

I want you to know that not everyone will like you, no matter how nice you are. Some people do not know how to truly love others, because they do not like themselves or because they do not know me. I myself have felt the pain of people not loving me. I know it hurts. And when you are sad, so am I. You can be sure that I will never reject you. You are a treasure to me and I am always with you wherever you are. When someone hurts you, I will always be here to heal your tender heart. So pray for those who do not like you and let me work in their hearts too.

Love,
Your King who loves you just the way you are

....

Praise be to God, who has not rejected my prayer or withheld his love from me!

PSALM 66:20, NIV

When I Am Hurting

Dear God, it really hurts my feelings when someone treats me mean or says they don't like me. Please help me to love them and pray for them anyway. Heal my hurting heart and help me feel your love. In Jesus' name I pray, amen.

When Friends Fight

Dear Lovely One of Mine,

All friends get mad at each other sometimes. But there is a right way and a wrong way to express your anger. When you feel angry, the first thing you should do is come to your King and tell me why you are mad. Then you must pray for the person you're mad at. If you will pray for your friend, I will help you to have the heart of a princess. I'll help you to speak to your friend with honesty and kindness. When people yell and say things to hurt each other, it breaks my heart and it never makes anyone feel better. If you have said something unkind to a friend, go and ask their forgiveness today.

Love,
Your King who always speaks the truth with love

Kind words are like honey—sweet to the soul and healthy for the body.

PROVERBS 16:24

Teach Me to Speak Kindly

Dear God, forgive me for speaking unkind words to my friends and family. I so want to act more like your daughter. Please help me to speak kind words and still be honest about my feelings. Thank you that you're always here to help me. In Jesus' name I pray, amen.

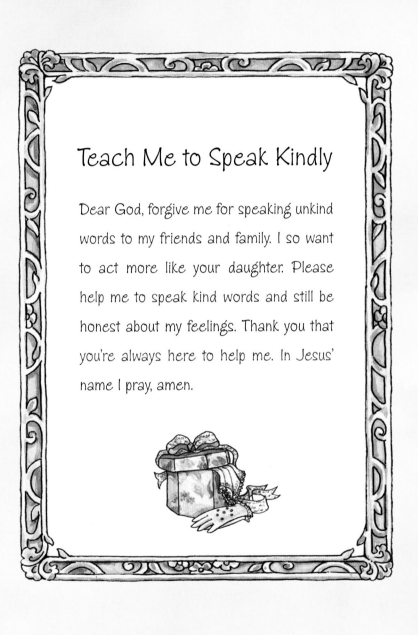

A Thankful Heart

Dear Princess,

A thankful heart is a happy heart. But there is a secret to keeping a thankful heart, even when things get hard or you don't get what you hoped for. The secret is to sing to me. The apostle Paul learned this in a dark, ugly jail. He had been arrested for telling people about my love for them. But Paul did not complain. Instead, he sang songs of praise to me with his friend Silas. My heart was glad! I shook the earth so hard that their chains fell off and the prison doors broke open. If you will think about things that are good and lovely and sing to me, no matter what, I will always do something special!

   Love,

   Your King who holds the key to every door

....

Accompanied by trumpets, cymbals, and other instruments, they raised their voices and praised the LORD with these words: "He is so good! His faithful love endures forever!"

2 CHRONICLES 5:13

Put a Song in My Heart

Dear God, I don't always have a thankful heart. Please forgive me for being thankful only when I get what I want. Help me to be thankful all day, every day. And put a song in my heart to sing to you no matter what I am feeling. In Jesus' name I pray, amen.

Do Not Give Up

Dear Darling Daughter,

Don't give up when things get hard. David was just a little shepherd boy when I told him he would one day become king of Israel. He was excited that I had chosen him. But before he was crowned, a lot of bad things happened to David. Saul, who was king before him, was jealous of David and wanted to kill him, so David had to hide in caves to protect himself. But David did not give up. He kept praying and singing to me and making wise choices until it was time for him to be king. I have great things planned for you too, my princess. So keep praying and singing and making wise choices!

Love,

Your King who has a wonderful plan for your life

....

"For I know the plans I have for you," says the LORD.
"They are plans for good and not for disaster,
to give you a future and a hope."

JEREMIAH 29:11

I Want to Always Be Your Girl

Dear God, I know your plan for my life is the very best. Make me ready for anything you want me to do. Help me to always be faithful and never give up. I love you and I want to always be your girl. In Jesus' name I pray, amen.

Do Not Tease

Dearest Princess,

Don't make fun of others by teasing them. A true princess cares how other people feel. Think of how sad or mad you feel when someone teases you! Remember, my love, you are representing me, your King, to lots of people who do not yet know me. So be careful not to be mean or unkind to anyone. Show them instead how much I care and how much I love them. If you will ask me, I can help you to see other people the way I do. When I open your eyes and let you see how every person is so very special to me, my love will begin to bubble up inside you until it overflows to everyone you meet!

Love,
Your King who lives in you

....

For everything we know about God's Word is summed up
in a single sentence: Love others as you love yourself.

GALATIANS 5:14, THE MESSAGE

Lord, Change My Heart

Dear God, I am so sorry for the times when I have teased others and hurt their feelings. I want to act like your princess by treating everyone special. Help me love others the way that you love them. Help me to never tease anyone again. In Jesus' name I pray, amen.

In Times of Sickness

Dear Daughter,

Sometimes the people we love get sick. I know this is hard for you. There are many reasons for sickness, my child. It is a time to take care of the ones you love and to show them your love by helping out in any way you can. One very important way you can help is to pray for those who are sick. Many times I will touch those who are sick and make them well. Sometimes I will take them home to Heaven to be with me. But you can trust me to know what is best for all my children. And when you do not feel well, remember, I will always be with you, my precious one.

Love,
Your King and your healer

....

The LORD nurses them when they are sick
and eases their pain and discomfort.

PSALM 41:3

You Are My Healer

Dear God, it's hard for me to see my family or friends feeling sick. Please heal them and comfort them when they do not feel good. And show me how to help them. In Jesus' name I pray, amen.

Angels Watching Over You

Dear Princess of Mine,

I have sent my angels to watch over you. Angels are not make-believe, my child. They are very real and very near! Do not be afraid. My angels are messengers and mighty warriors. I sent them into the lions' den to protect Daniel. I sent my angel into a furnace filled with fire to protect my children Shadrach, Meshach, and Abednego. I sent an entire army of angels in chariots of fire to protect my prophet Elisha. And I will do the same for you, my daughter. I am just as powerful today as a thousand years ago. My protection is yours for the asking, because you are my princess.

Love,
Your King who commands the angels of Heaven

God will command his angels to protect you wherever you go.

PSALM 91:11, CEV

Send Your Angels to Protect Me

Dear God, thank you for creating the angels of Heaven. Thank you for sending your angels to protect me. I am so blessed to be under your protection and to call you my Father. I love being your princess! In Jesus' name I pray, amen.

Honor the Elderly

Dear Daughter,

Many years ago your grandma and grandpa were young like you, but they have since grown older and wiser. Older people deserve your respect because they have lived a long time and learned a great many important things about life. If you will sit with your grandma and grandpa and listen carefully, they will share with you valuable treasures of wisdom and truth and teach you how to make good choices. You can show honor to older people by listening to them and by helping and serving them in any way you can. It makes my heart glad to see you treat the elderly with honor. If you will do what I ask, you will bless your King very much.

Love,
Your King who cares for the young and the old

....

"Show your fear of God by standing up in the presence of elderly people and showing respect for the aged."

LEVITICUS 19:32

Help Me to Honor
My Grandparents

Dear God, I want to please you by honoring older people like my grandpa and grandma. Please help me to treat the elderly with love and kindness. Help me to learn from older people. And show me what I can do to help them. In Jesus' name I pray, amen.

Dress like Royalty

My Princess,

You are a daughter of the King. Because you are my chosen princess you should dress modestly every day. You are mine, and in my eyes you are pure and precious. I want everyone to see that you are mine by the way you dress. Sadly, there are a lot of girls who do not think about me when they get dressed in the morning. They wear clothes that do not cover their bodies or that show their bodies in an immodest way. I do not want you to dress like them. Instead, pray to me about what clothes you should wear. Keep your body covered and be my model to others.

Love,
Your King who will dress you in my glory

....

I want women to be modest in their appearance....
For women who claim to be devoted to God should make
themselves attractive by the good things they do.

1 TIMOTHY 2:9–10

Dress Me like a Princess

Dear God, I want to look like a princess. Help me pick out clothes that please you. Teach me how to make myself attractive by doing good things in your name. Thank you for choosing me to represent you. In Jesus' name I pray, amen.

Friends Are a Gift

Dear Child,

I want to talk to you about friends, my love. I have given you friends as a gift to enjoy. So treat your friends the way you would treat a brand-new toy on Christmas morning. Take very special care of your friends and show them that they are precious to you. If you will do this, you will keep those friends for a long time. But if you treat your friends like an old toy you do not care about anymore, then they will treat you the same way and they will no longer want to be around you. A good friend is a gift to be treasured. If you ask, I can help you be a good friend.

Love,
Your King and your friend

A friend loves at all times.

PROVERBS 17:17, NIV

I Want to Be a Good Friend

Dear God, please forgive me for the times when I haven't treated my friends kindly. I want to learn how to be a good friend. You have shown me that I am precious to you; help me to show my friends that they are precious to me. In Jesus' name I pray, amen.

Sweet Dreams, My Love

Dear Princess,

I will be watching over you while you sleep. I want to bless you with sweet sleep, my love, so be sure you talk to me each night when you go to bed. You can sing a song to me before you fall asleep. You know how I love to hear you sing! Do not be afraid of the darkness, because I am the Light in the dark that will protect you while you are resting your eyes. I never sleep and I never take my eyes off my daughter—not even for a moment. So have sweet dreams, my little princess, and snuggle up in my love. Good night, daughter. I love you very much.

Love,
Your King who is always by your side

....

When you lie down, you shall not be afraid;
yes, you shall lie down, and your sleep shall be sweet.

PROVERBS 3:24, AMP

You Are My Light in the Night

Dear God, I'm so happy to know that you are always watching over me. With you by my side, I will not be afraid. Please help me to sleep well and give me good dreams. Good night, Father. In Jesus' name I pray, amen.

Christmas Day

Dear Princess of Mine,

Christmas is my gift of love to the world. Always remember the true story of Christmas. My chosen child Mary was also my very special princess. I picked her to give birth to Jesus, my only Son. Young Mary was a little scared at first, but she did not give up hope and she trusted me. When it was time to bring baby Jesus into the world, there was no hospital and no soft bed for Mary to rest in. So she gave birth in a stable, surrounded by barn animals. That blessed night was the most special time the world has ever known. Because of my Son, you will get to spend forever with me. Merry Christmas, my love.

Love,
Your King who gave you his Son

"I bring you good news of great joy that will be for all the people. Today in the town of David a Savior has been born to you; he is Christ the Lord."

LUKE 2:10–11, NIV

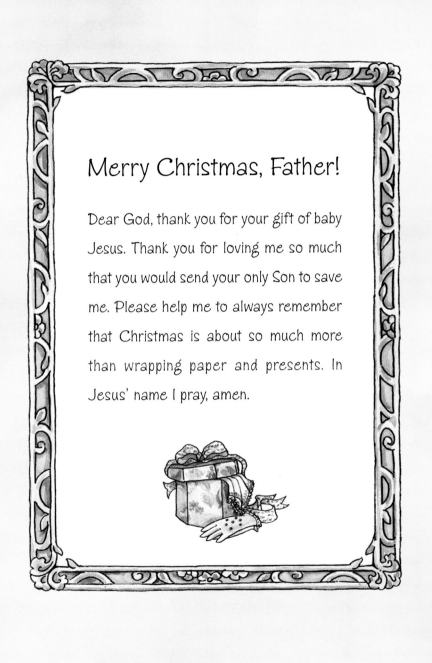

Merry Christmas, Father!

Dear God, thank you for your gift of baby Jesus. Thank you for loving me so much that you would send your only Son to save me. Please help me to always remember that Christmas is about so much more than wrapping paper and presents. In Jesus' name I pray, amen.

My Word Is True

Dearest Daughter,

Every word I have written to you in the Bible is true. All the stories of miracles and wonders really happened. And just as I placed a rainbow in the sky as a promise to Noah, every promise I have made in the Bible is also for you, my princess. I have written there all the secrets of how to live and act like my princess. Every time you read the Bible, you will find a new treasure of truth to hide in your heart. I am the same God who parted the Red Sea for Moses and the children of Israel. I am the same God who created the heavens and the earth. I am your God, and you can trust my Word.

Love,
Your King who keeps his promises

....

I have placed my rainbow in the clouds. It is the sign of my permanent promise to you and to all the earth.

GENESIS 9:13

I Love to Read the Bible

Dear God, thank you for always keeping your promises. Thank you for the Bible. I love to read about all the wonderful things my Daddy in Heaven has done— and about all the things you will do for me because I am yours. In Jesus' name I pray, amen.

Try, Try Again

Dear Daughter,

Never be afraid of trying again just because something is hard to do. Sometimes it takes more than one try to learn something new. When you're first learning to ride a new bike, you may fall off many times before you are able to ride by yourself. Whatever you face in this life, I will always be here to take care of you. I will be with you as you learn and grow and explore. And I will help you get up again every time you fall or fail. Remember, a true princess may fall occasionally, but she will always try again until she learns what she has set her mind to do.

Love,
Your King who is here to catch you when you fall

....

Even if good people fall seven times,
they will get back up. But when trouble strikes
the wicked, that's the end of them.

PROVERBS 24:16, CEV

I Will Trust in You

Dear God, sometimes it's hard for me to try new things. It's especially hard when I try a new thing and cannot do it the first time. Thank you that you will always help me to get back up when I fall and to try again. In Jesus' name I pray, amen.

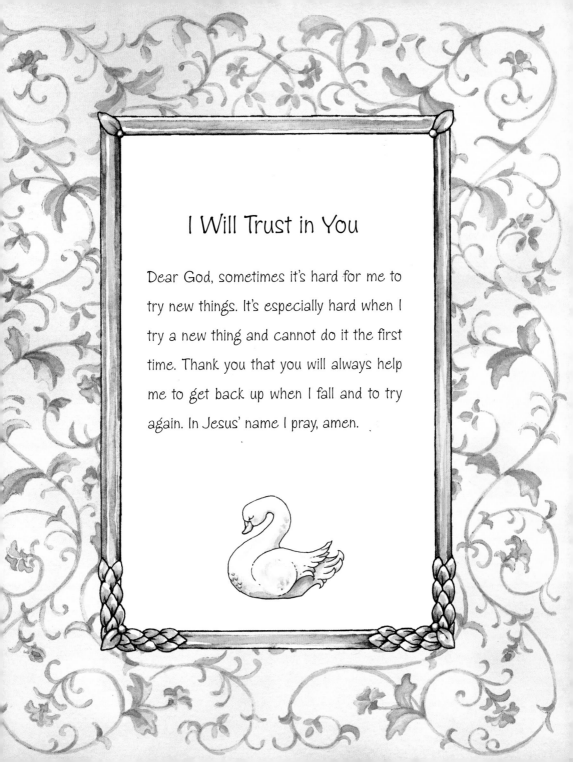

Always Do Your Best

Dear Chosen One,

Everywhere you go, in everything you do, you show the world whom you belong to. When others watch you, they are seeing me because I am in your heart and my Spirit is with you. Because this is true I am going to ask you to do something important for me: I want you to always do your best, no matter what you are doing. Whether you are working or playing or learning, always do the best you can do. Sometimes you will make mistakes, and that's okay. But I want you to try your hardest. You will set a good example for others by giving your best effort. Remember, I have chosen you to show others how to live as my children.

Love,
Your King who is proud of his princess

....

Set an example for other followers by what you say and do,
as well as by your love, faith, and purity.

1 TIMOTHY 4:12, CEV

Help Me to Do My Best

Dear God, please forgive me for the times when I have not done the best I can do. Help me to remember I am yours and that others see you when they see me. Help me to give my very best in everything I do. In Jesus' name I pray, amen.

A Princess Does Not Brag

My Blessed Daughter,

I have given you special gifts and talents. I have blessed you so that you can bless others. I did not give you these gifts so that you may boast or brag. When you brag about yourself, you make others feel bad. I want you to be glad in your heart for the things you have and the special talents I have given you. I love to give you things, my girl, but don't ever try to make yourself look important. Don't keep talking about the things you own or what you can do. Instead, tell me how thankful you are, and ask me how you can use your belongings and talents to help others.

Love,
Your King who gives every good gift

....

"Let him who boasts boast about this: that he understands and knows me, that I am the LORD, who exercises kindness, justice and righteousness on earth, for in these I delight."
JEREMIAH 9:23–24, NIV

I Will Not Boast or Brag

Dear God, I am so sorry for bragging about the gifts you've given me. Help me to use my belongings and talents to make others happy. And the only thing I will brag about is how good you are to me. In Jesus' name I pray, amen.

Love People the Way I Do

Dear Special Daughter,

Let me open your eyes to see the world of people the way your King does. I made every person on the earth, and I love each and every one of them just the way they are. People are all different because I made them that way. That is why I want you to treat everyone the same, whether they are old or young, rich or poor, sick or healthy, black or white. Be careful, my princess, to accept people for who they are. Ask me and I will help you learn to appreciate people who are different from you. When you learn to see people the way I see them, you will begin to love them the way I love them.

Love,
Your King who made you to love others

"Didn't the same God who made me, make them?
Aren't we all made of the same stuff, equals before God?"

Job 31:15, The Message

You Made Us All

Dear God, thank you for making the many wonderful kinds of people in the world. Please help me to love them all just the way they are, no matter how different they may seem. Thank you too that I am unique and different from everyone else. In Jesus' name I pray, amen.

Meet Me at Church

Dear Princess,

You gladden my heart when you come to meet with me. When you make time to go to church and learn more about our special relationship, my heart is filled with joy! I love to see my children gather together to sing my praises, read the Bible, and pray for each other. You may not always understand everything the grown-ups at church try to teach you about me, but you can be sure that my Holy Spirit will help you to know me more and more as you grow. I will always send my Spirit to be with you in a very special way when you spend time with people who love me.

Love,
Your King who loves to meet with you

....

My soul thirsts for God, for the living God.
When can I go and meet with God?

PSALM 42:2, NIV

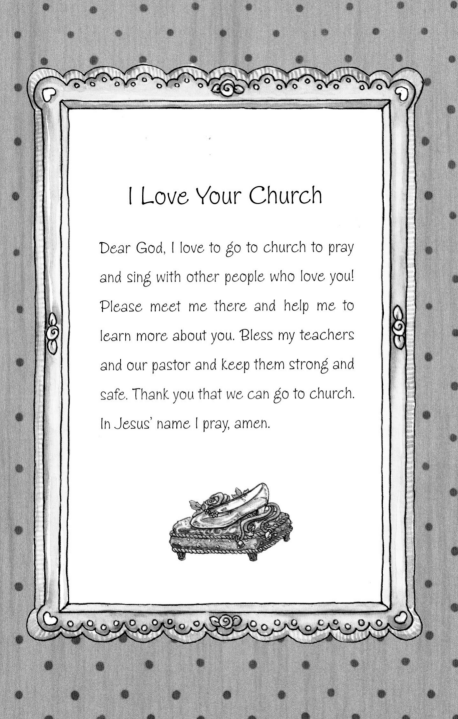

I Love Your Church

Dear God, I love to go to church to pray and sing with other people who love you! Please meet me there and help me to learn more about you. Bless my teachers and our pastor and keep them strong and safe. Thank you that we can go to church. In Jesus' name I pray, amen.

Have Faith, My Child

Dear Daughter,

Faith means trusting me, even when life gets hard. Sometimes, my love, you may feel like I am not with you when bad things happen. But I am *always* with you. When Samson was blinded by the Philistines and thrown into prison, he probably thought I had forgotten him. But I still had great plans for Samson to rescue my people and to show the Philistines that I am the one true God. And so with one mighty push, Samson destroyed the Philistine temple. I see everything, and I will punish those who hurt my children. You can know in your heart that I will always keep my promise.

Love,
Your King who is always with you

....

*Faith makes us sure of what we hope for and
gives us proof of what we cannot see. It was their faith
that made our ancestors pleasing to God.*

Hebrews 11:1–2, CEV

Strengthen My Faith

Dear God, help me to have faith in you, no matter what. Sometimes when bad things happen I forget that you are always with me. When I am sad or angry or frightened, please help me to feel you near and to trust in you. In Jesus' name I pray, amen.

Do Not Be Jealous

Dear Princess,

Jealousy is something you feel inside when someone else has something you want or something you don't have. You might be jealous of another person's talent. Or you might be jealous of a brother or sister and the attention they're getting from your mom and dad. Jealousy can be a very dangerous thing because it makes you ungrateful for the things you have. And jealousy may cause you to act unkindly toward a friend or family member. But I am here to help you when you feel this way. So pray and confess your jealous feelings to your Daddy in Heaven. I will change your heart and help you to be happy and thankful for all that I've given you.

Love,
Your King who gives you everything you need

....

You are jealous of one another and quarrel with each other....
You are acting like people who don't belong to the Lord.

1 CORINTHIANS 3:3

Forgive Me for Being Jealous

Dear God, sometimes I'm jealous of my friends who can do things that I can't do. Sometimes I'm jealous of people who have more toys or nicer clothes than I have. Please forgive me and help me to keep a princess heart that is always thankful. In Jesus' name I pray, amen.

My Patient Princess

Dearest Daughter,

Patience means waiting without complaining for something to happen that you *really want* to happen. Waiting can be so hard, but if you keep the right attitude while waiting, then just thinking about the wonderful thing to come can be as special in your heart as when it actually happens. When I knit you together in your mother's tummy, I couldn't wait to see you come into the world! When you feel yourself growing impatient, I want you to first pray. Then I want you to use your imagination to dream about the thing you are excited to see happen. And I will send you your heart's desire at just the perfect time.

Love,
Your King who brings good things to those who wait

....

We also pray that you will be strengthened with his glorious power so that you will have all the patience and endurance you need.

Colossians 1:11

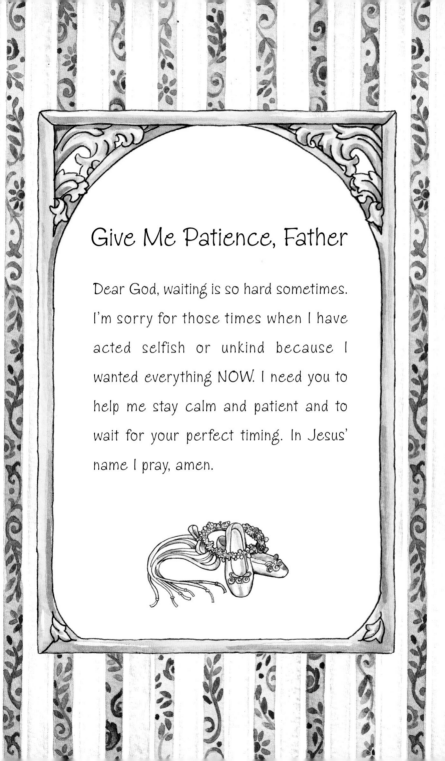

Give Me Patience, Father

Dear God, waiting is so hard sometimes. I'm sorry for those times when I have acted selfish or unkind because I wanted everything NOW. I need you to help me stay calm and patient and to wait for your perfect timing. In Jesus' name I pray, amen.

Telling the Truth

Dear Princess,

I will never lie to you, my love. You can always trust my Word. You are my chosen princess, and I want others to know they can also trust *you* to tell the truth. Sometimes things happen that will make it hard for you to do that. For example, if you have done something wrong, you may be afraid to tell the truth about it. Other times you might be tempted to lie to make someone like you more. But telling a lie will never feel good in your heart, because your heart is where I live! I want my daughter to always tell the truth. So when you are tempted to tell a lie, pray and I will help you be truthful instead.

Love,
Your King who always tells the truth

"If you want a happy life and good days, keep your tongue from speaking evil, and keep your lips from telling lies."

1 PETER 3:10

I Will Not Tell a Lie

Dear God, I am so sorry for the times when I have not told the truth. Please help me to always talk like your princess. Help me never to tell a lie. I want to be a person that others trust. In Jesus' name I pray, amen.

Jesus Died for You

Dear Daughter of Mine,

More than two thousand years ago I sent my only Son to earth to teach people about me and about Heaven and about my love. Jesus loved you so much that he chose to die on a cross to erase every bad choice you ever made. Because he did this, anyone who believes that Jesus is my Son and asks him into their hearts can become a child of the King. My precious daughter, if you have not already asked Jesus into your heart, I want you to do it now so that you can be with me forever. If you have already asked Jesus into your heart, then shout praises to him and thank him for the gift of eternal life!

Love,
Your King who gave his only Son to die for you

....

"For God so loved the world that he gave his only Son, so that everyone who believes in him will not perish but have eternal life."

JOHN 3:16

Come into My Heart, Jesus

Dear Jesus, thank you for dying on the cross for me. I want you to come into my heart and forgive me for every bad thing I have ever done. I want to live for you from now on. I love you, Jesus! In your name I pray, amen.

Telling People About Jesus

Dear Chosen One,

You can help someone get to Heaven! Do you know how? By telling people about Jesus. There are many ways you can tell others the good news about my Son. Start by praying for people who do not know Jesus. Then ask me and I will show you how to tell them about becoming a Christian. I will always answer your prayers for people who need to know me. Just by doing kind things for these people and letting them know that you are praying for them, you will be a blessing to them. And I will bless you for telling them about me! And then all will see that you are my little princess and I am your King.

Love,
Your King who has good news for you to share

....

God has brought you out of darkness into his marvelous light.
Now you must tell all the wonderful things that he has done.

1 PETER 2:9, CEV

I Want to Spread the Good News

Dear God, I love you so much. I want everyone to know you. Please give me the words to tell others about Jesus, and remind me to pray for the people who don't know you yet. In Jesus' name I pray, amen.

Open Your Gift

My Princess,

You have a very special gift that I have placed inside of you. Do you know what gift that is? It is something you can do very, very well. As you grow you will learn more about this special gift. You will learn that some things are easy for you and make you feel good when you're doing them. There will be other things your friends do better. Remember, you do not have to try to be like anyone else. I want you to be thankful for the way I created you. Then I can help you open that precious gift inside of you. I have a wonderful purpose for your life. Ask me, and I will help you find it.

Love,
Your King who is preparing you for something special

....

God has given each of us the ability
to do certain things well.

ROMANS 12:6

Thank You for My Gift

Dear God, thank you for placing a special gift inside me. Help me find my gift, and please show me how to use it to help people. Help me be everything you want me to be. In Jesus' name I pray, amen.

Presents in Heaven

Dear Daughter,

One day you will come to live with me in Heaven. I am very excited because I have so many presents to give you when you get here. Did you know that every time you do or say something kind to others just because you want them to know you are mine, I am preparing another gift for you in Heaven? Remember, my love: Even if no one else notices the sweet things you do for them, I see everything you do. And for all the kindness you do in secret, I will reward you openly and richly in Heaven. I want you to know in your heart that I am so very proud of you.

Love,
Your King who has wonderful surprises waiting for you

....

*"No eye has seen, no ear has heard, and no mind has imagined
what God has prepared for those who love him."*

1 Corinthians 2:9

You See Everything I Do

Dear God, thank you for seeing me when no one else does. Thank you for my presents. I cannot wait to open them someday! Help me to always act like your daughter—even when no one is looking. In Jesus' name I pray, amen.

Death Is Not the End

My Chosen One,

I never want you to be afraid of death, my daughter, because death is not the end of life for my children. It is only the beginning of their *forever* life. All those that have loved me and have died are with me now in Heaven. Remember this truth: When you leave this earth, you also will be with me forever. I know you miss the precious ones who have died, but I promise you will see them again, my love. If you will talk to me when you feel sad, I will heal your heart and remind you that someday we will all live happily ever after, together as one family in Heaven.

Love,

Your King who is preparing a home for all my children

Jesus told her, "I am the resurrection and the life. Those who believe in me, even though they die like everyone else, will live again."

JOHN 11:25

Comfort Me, Lord

Dear God, I do feel sad when someone I love has died. Help me remember that everyone who loves you will live with you after they die. Help me remember that I will see them all in Heaven one day. In Jesus' name I pray, amen.

A Home in Heaven

Dearest Princess,

I am preparing for you the most beautiful place you have ever seen! In Heaven the streets are made of gold, and the sea is like diamond crystals sparkling in the light of my love. In your heavenly home no one will be able to hurt you or any of my precious children ever again. You will never be afraid there or cry another tear. No one will ever have to die again, and all the bad things that happened in this life will be gone forever. Think about your home in Heaven, my love. You are here on this earth for a little while to tell others I love them. Then we will sing and celebrate together forever and ever!

Love,

Your King who loves you now and forever

....

He will live with them, and they will be his people. God himself will be with them. He will remove all of their sorrows, and there will be no more death or sorrow or crying or pain.

REVELATION 21:3–4

Happily Ever After

Dear God, thank you! Thank you so much for my beautiful forever home in Heaven. I am so glad you chose me to be your princess for now and forever. Help me to always live and act like I belong to you. In Jesus' name I pray, amen.

About the Author and Illustrator

SHERI ROSE SHEPHERD is the author of the popular His Princess™ series. A former Mrs. United States, Sheri Rose is an anointed teacher who has served as keynote speaker at Women of Virtue conferences and as the national spokesperson for Teen Challenge (1994–1998). She is passionate about drawing princesses of all ages closer to God and showing them how much they are loved by their King. Sheri Rose has been married for eighteen years and has two beautiful children.

LISA MARIE BROWNING attended Philadelphia College of Art and has been illustrating children's books for seven of her twenty-two years as an artist.

Scripture References

A Devotional Gift Book
Moms Will Treasure Too!

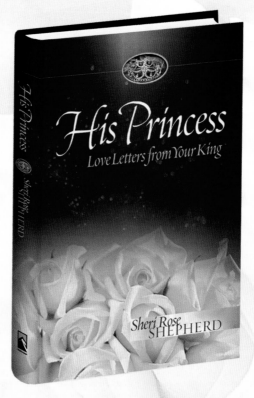

Moms, give yourself the gift of hearing His voice speaking directly to you in these beautiful scriptural love letters from your King. Let your soul soak in His love as each letter reminds you WHO you are, WHY you are here, and HOW much you are loved.

I have many devotional books, but very few have found their way into my morning quiet-time ritual. But from the first day I began His Princess *I knew this was a book I wanted to read every day. Encouraging and insightful, this book reminds me how special I am to my Lord. I love this book!*

—Tricia Goyer, amazon.com reviewer

His Princess™
MINISTRIES

We would love to hear from you!

If you would like to contact Sheri Rose, schedule her to speak at your next event, or request information about His Princess™ Conferences, please visit www.HisPrincess.com.

Note for women's ministry directors and pastors' wives: Please call (602) 407-8789 to receive a free sample teaching on DVD.

Find out more ways to tell your little girl she is God's princess!

- His Little Princess Conferences
- His Little Princess Tea Sets
- His Little Princess Birthday Party Packs
- His Little Princess Crowns and Jewelry
- His Little Princess News

Visit www.HisPrincess.com or call 602-407-8789 for a free catalog.